DISCOVER DOGS WITH THE AMERICAN CANINE ASSOCIATION

I LIKE POMERANIANS!

Linda Bozzo

It is the mission of the American Canine Association (ACA) to provide registered dog owners with the educational support needed for raising, training, showing, and breeding the healthiest pets expected by responsible pet owners throughout the world. Through our activities and services, we encourage and support the dog world in order to promote best-known husbandry standards as well as to ensure that the voice and needs of our customers are quickly and properly addressed.

Our continued support, commitment, and direction are guided by our customers, including veterinary, legal, and legislative advisors. ACA aims to provide the most efficient, cooperative, and courteous service to our customers and strives to set the standard for education and problem solving for all who depend on our services.

For more information, please visit www.acacanines.com, email customerservice@acadogs.com, phone 1-800-651-8332, or write to the American Canine Association at PO Box 121107, Clermont, FL 34712.

Published in 2019 by Enslow Publishing, LLC.
101 W. 23rd Street, Suite 240, New York, NY 10011

Library of Congress Cataloging-in-Publication Data

Names: Bozzo, Linda, author.
Title: I like pomeranians! / Linda Bozzo.
Description: New York : Enslow Publishing, 2019. | Series: Discover dogs with the American Canine Association | Audience: K to Grade 3. | Includes bibliographical references and index.
Identifiers: LCCN 2018005417 | ISBN 9781978501904 (library bound) | ISBN 9781978502598 (paperback) | ISBN 9781978502604 (6 pack)
Subjects: LCSH: Pomeranian dog—Juvenile literature.
Classification: LCC SF429.P8 B69 2019 | DDC 636.76—dc23
LC record available at https://lccn.loc.gov/2018005417

Printed in the United States of America

To Our Readers: We have done our best to make sure all websites in this book were active and appropriate when we went to press. However, the author and the publisher have no control over and assume no liability for the material available on those websites or on any websites they may link to. Any comments or suggestions can be sent by email to customerservice@enslow.com.

Photo Credits: Cover, p. 1 Suti Stock Photo/Shutterstock.com; p. 3 (left), Leeyakorn06/Shutterstock.com; p. 3 (right) pimonphotography/Shutterstock.com; p. 5 Pavel_D/Shutterstock.com; p. 6 thanai asawaroengchai/Shutterstock.com; p. 9 © iStockphoto.com/MangoStar_Studio; p. 10 Dragon Images/Shutterstock.com; p. 13 (left) pattarawat/Shutterstock.com; p 13 (right) graphicphoto/Thinkstock/(collar), Luisa Leal Photography/Shutterstock.com (bed), gvictoria/Shutterstock.com (brush), exopixel/Shutterstock.com (dishes), © iStockphoto.com/Lisa Thornberg (leash, toys); p. 14 Yemets/Shutterstock.com; p. 17 © iStockphoto.com/sutichak; p. 18 Oksana Kuzmina/Shutterstock.com; p. 19 KPG Payless2/Shutterstock.com; p. 21 sommart sombutwanitkul/Shutterstock.com.

Enslow Publishing
101 W. 23rd Street
Suite 240
New York, NY 10011
USA
enslow.com

CONTENTS

IS A POMERANIAN RIGHT FOR YOU?

Pomeranians don't mind playing indoor games. If you live in an apartment or you don't have a fenced yard, a Pomeranian might be right for you.

Due to their small size, Pomeranians must be handled with extra care.

A DOG OR A PUPPY?

Pomeranians are always ready to learn, but house-training can be hard. If you do not have time to train a puppy, you may want an older Pomeranian instead.

Training sessions should be kept short and fun.

LOVING YOUR POMERANIAN

Pomeranians are playful and curious. Love your Pomeranian by teaching him tricks. He will also love to cuddle on your lap.

Pomeranians were bred in Germany as pets for royalty.

EXERCISE

Due to their small size, Pomeranians don't need much exercise. An afternoon walk on a leash or a romp around the yard is all they need. This lively little dog enjoys playing games like fetch.

Keep in mind that Pomeranians don't do well in the heat. Be sure to keep them cool on a hot day!

FEEDING YOUR POMERANIAN

Pomeranians can be fed wet or dry dog food. Ask a veterinarian (vet), a doctor for animals, which food is best for your dog and how much to feed her.

Give your Pomeranian fresh, clean water every day.

Remember to keep your dog's food and water dishes clean. Dirty dishes can make a dog sick.

Do not feed your dog people food. It can make her sick.

Your new dog will need:

a collar with a tag

a bed

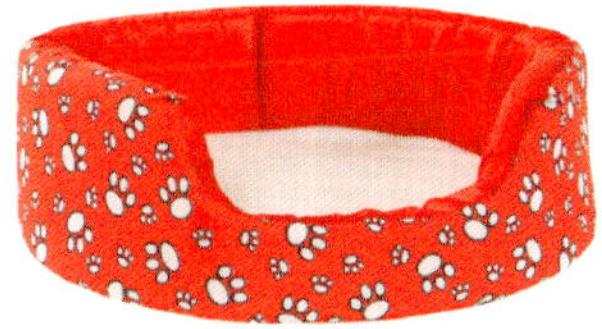

a brush

food and water dishes

a leash

toys

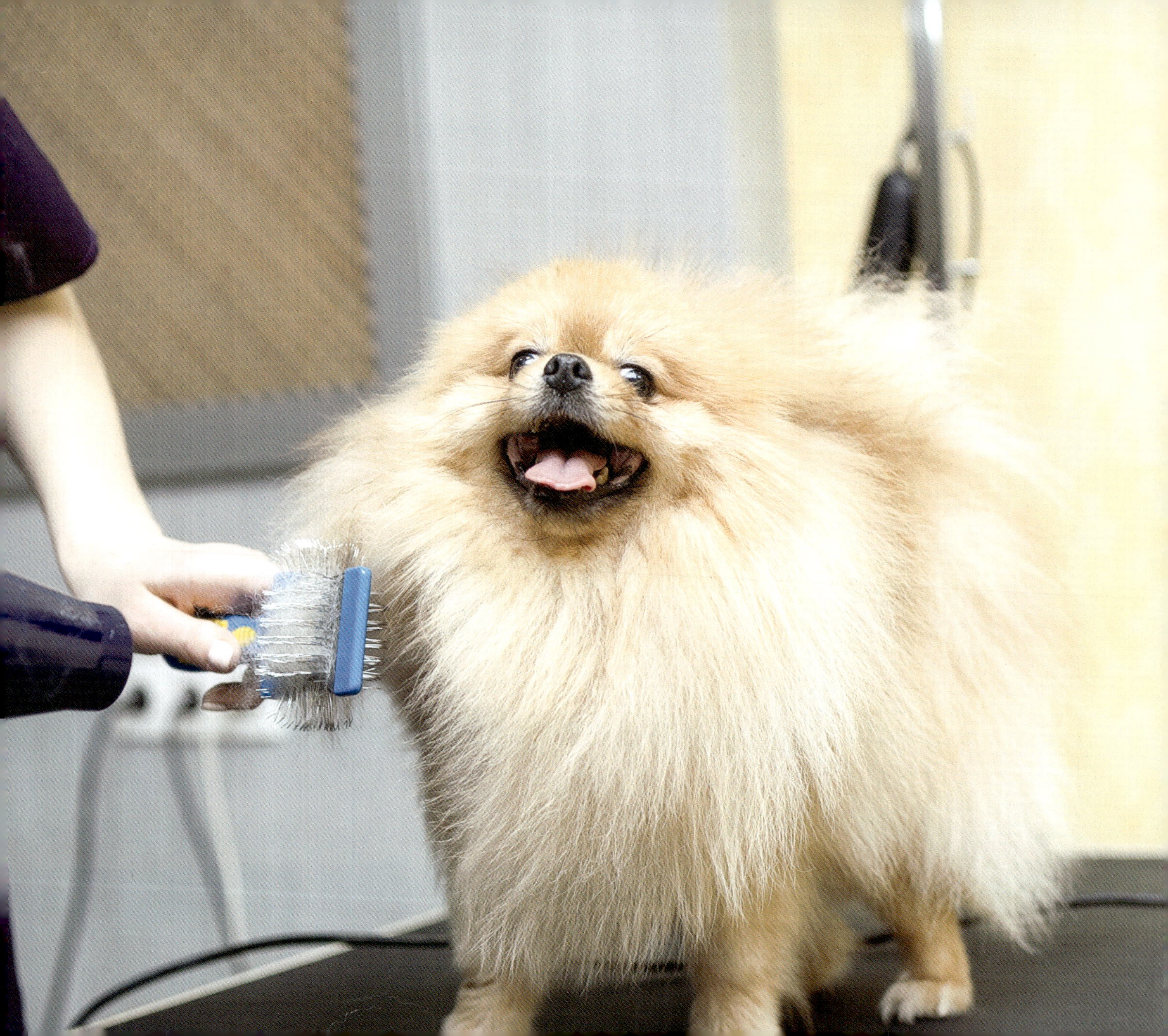

GROOMING

Pomeranians shed. This means their hair falls out. They need to be brushed often. Baths will help to keep your dog clean. Make sure you use shampoo made specially for dogs. Your Pomeranian will need trips to the groomer for hair trimming.

Your Pomeranian's nails will need to be clipped. A vet or groomer can show you how. Your dog's ears should be cleaned, and his teeth should be brushed by an adult.

WHAT YOU SHOULD KNOW

With their loud bark, Pomeranians make good watchdogs.

Due to their small size, Pomeranians are easily injured. They don't seem to know how small they are. For this reason, they need to be watched around larger dogs.

You will need to take your new dog to the vet for a checkup. He will need shots, called **vaccinations**, and yearly checkups to keep him healthy. If you think your dog may be sick or hurt, call your vet.

A GOOD FRIEND

Small size, big eyes, and fluffy fur make Pomeranians as cute as they are fun. Whether playing or cuddling on your lap, your Pomeranian will be a good friend for many years.

This small breed can live as long as sixteen years.

NOTE TO PARENTS

It is important to consider having your dog spayed or neutered when the dog is young. Spaying and neutering are operations that prevent unwanted puppies and can help improve the overall health of your dog.

It is also a good idea to microchip your dog, in case he or she gets lost. A vet will implant a microchip under the skin containing an identification number that can be scanned at a vet's office or animal shelter. The microchip registry is contacted, and the company uses the ID number to look up your information from a database.

Some towns require licenses for dogs, so be sure to check with your town clerk.

For more information, speak with a vet.

There are many dogs, young and old, waiting to be adopted from animal shelters and rescue groups.

Words to Know

fetch To go after a toy and bring it back.

groomer A person who bathes and brushes dogs.

leash A chain or strap that attaches to the dog's collar.

romp Rough play.

shed When a dog's hair falls out so new hair can grow.

vaccinations Shots that dogs need to stay healthy.

veterinarian (vet) A doctor for animals.

Read About Dogs

Books

Brown, Domini. *Pomeranians*. Minneapolis, MN: Bellwether Media, 2017.

Gray, Susan Heinrichs. *Pomeranians*. New York, NY: AV2 by Weigl, 2017.

Morey, Alan. *Pomeranians*. North Mankato, MN: Capstone Press, 2017.

Websites

American Canine Association Inc., Kids Corner
www.acakids.com
Visit the official website of the American Canine Association.

National Geographic for Kids, Pet Central
kids.nationalgeographic.com/explore/pet-central
Learn more about dogs and other pets at the official site of the National Geographic Society for Kids.

INDEX